How
To
Advertise
Yourself

How To Advertise Yourself

**Five Basic Steps to "Selling"
Your Appearance,
Your Thoughts,
Your Words,
and Your Experience to
Any Individual
or Group**

by Maxwell Sackheim

Foreword by Forrest Wallace Cato

Macmillan Publishing Co., Inc.   New York

Collier Macmillan Publishers   London

Macmillan Publishing Co., Inc.
866 Third Avenue, New York, N.Y.   10022

Collier Macmillan Canada, Ltd.

Library of Congress Catalog Card Number: 78-50787

Printed in the United States of America

printing number
2 3 4 5 6 7 8 9 10

Library of Congress Cataloging in Publication Data

Sackheim, Maxwell
  How to advertise yourself.

  1. Success. 2. Advertising. 3. Selling.
4. Interpersonal relations. I. Title.
HF5386.S23   131'.32   78-50787
ISBN   0-02-927680-2

Contents

5

Foreword

As he tells it himself, the first ad Maxwell Sackheim ever wrote was written in the snow. The advertising company he worked for in Chicago, in 1905, was located in a building overlooking Michigan Avenue and the lakefront park. He noticed that some boys playing tag in the park had formed a distinct sculptured pattern by trampling the snow. Sackheim went down and, in the fresh snow beneath his boss's office window, trampled his company's initials. His boss saw him from his window, high above in his office. When Sackheim returned, his boss called him in, smiled, and increased Max's salary from $3.00 to $3.50 a week.

After six years in that agency, Max rewrote a Sears, Roebuck ad and mailed it to the Sears advertising manager (whose name he didn't even know!) and was offered a job in the advertising department of that giant merchandising establishment (a giant even way back in 1913). In 1914, on a trip to New York, Sackheim met Harry Scherman, a brilliant copywriter; from their meeting developed the Sackheim & Scherman advertising agency and eventually the now famous Book-of-the-Month Club.

Their extracurricular activities started with the Little Leather Library (a forerunner of the Pocket Books idea), which the partners launched with an investment of $300. The first direct advertisement for the Little Leather Library, written by Sackheim—"a genius in this type of advertising," said Harry Scherman—appeared in *Pathfinder* magazine: "30 World's Great Classics for $2.98. Send no money. Pay when the postman delivers." From 1920 to 1924 this technique, in various forms, sold more than forty million books by mail.

Messrs. Sackheim & Scherman then proceeded to offer phonograph records by mail! In the first year of operation under the name National Music Lovers a million dollars' worth was sold. Up to that time, records had been primarily sold singly. The new mail-order company sold them in albums of eight records for $2.98. They included old-time American songs, sacred music, grand opera, and popular selections. The record business was great—but another great idea (radio) killed National Music Lovers.

In 1926, the Book-of-the-Month Club was formed by the partners while Sackheim & Scherman was also functioning with some twenty-five accounts and substantial billing. In 1928, Sackheim joined Brown Fence & Wire

8

Company of Cleveland, Ohio. After sixteen years of frustrating experience there, Sackheim returned to New York in 1944 to his first love—advertising—and with three accounts was back in the agency business at the age of fifty-three, practically "broke."

The number of giant enterprises Sackheim helped to guide during the various stages of his advertising career is utterly astonishing. For instance, he was one of two architects of the revolutionary promotion method that has been unsurpassed for getting maximum profits from mail-order sales of books. You know it as the Book-of-the-Month Club. Sackheim helped launch the American Express credit card and make it the foremost of its kind in the world. He created ads for many successful mail-order projects, successful not necessarily in terms of art or awards but outstanding in sales results. For instance, in 1918 he wrote an ad headlined "Do You Make These Mistakes in English?" This now classic ad ran for more than forty years with only minor changes. During those years the ad pulled and pulled, amassing profits for both the buyer and seller. This ad was immortalized in Julian Watkins' book *100 Greatest Advertisements* and is recognized as one of the great ads of all time.

Today the world's acknowledged advertising leaders consider Sackheim to be one of the few great masters of advertising, a proven creator of successful and outstanding advertising that causes products and money to be exchanged. As Pete Hoke, editor of *Direct Marketing*, said, "Maxwell Sackheim is the granddaddy of that rare breed of direct marketing genius who can look at nearly any selling situation, clearly detect and compose its right offer, direct it to the right people at the right time; then know that he's done it by collecting and analyzing concrete results." And Robert F. DeLay, president of Direct Mail/Marketing Association says: "You've heard of the 'Seven Deadly Advertising Mistakes.' The eighth would be to miss reading Max Sackheim's book! Maxwell Sackheim is an unusual man. You name it, and you will find that Max either initiated it, improved it, or sold it."

This book—*How To Advertise Yourself*—may bring you results you could not possibly hope to obtain without adopting, applying, and developing some of the methods so successfully used in "selling" other and far less worthy wares than YOU! Advertise YOURSELF in the right way and you will make the most of *what you* KNOW and *what you* ARE!

FORREST WALLACE CATO

How To Advertise Yourself

1 Introduction

After spending nearly seventy years almost totally involved in the business of planning and writing advertising, I am moved to transfer the accumulation of these seven decades of advertising experience from the selling of products and services to the selling of your own most important commodity—YOURSELF!

What is the secret of personal success in life? The ability to *sell yourself* to the rest of the world! Very few products or people are bought. Most successes are *sold*—and ADVERTISING, in one form or another, is the medium by which they are made known to "prospective customers."

This book is intended to help you "sell" your appearance, your thoughts, your words, and your experience to any individual or group. To do it—and I will show you how in this book—you must first grasp five tested principles of advertising: first, you must KNOW YOUR MERCHANDISE (yourself); second, you must ATTRACT FAVORABLE ATTENTION; third, you must present your thoughts to your "customers" in a way to KEEP 'EM INTERESTED; fourth, you must BE CONVINCING; and finally, as in any commercial advertising program, you must make every effort to GET ACTION in response to your appeal.

1. You must KNOW YOUR "MERCHANDISE" thoroughly. Analyze yourself as a PRODUCT; examine its good and bad points, its competition, and every conceivable reason your prospect should "buy" it in exchange for its cost. You must know yourself because you are the "merchandise" and as such you can never—not for a single moment in any day of your life—get away from yourself. And you must *like* yourself, for if you do not like yourself you will not like others. You must *respect* yourself, for if you do not respect yourself you will not respect others. And if you do not like and respect yourself, others will neither like nor respect you. Resolve that you will, from now on, have an increased respect and esteem for the one person with whom you will inevitably have to live and get along with on this earth—YOURSELF. If you think this sounds like saying be egotistical, let me warn you that you will never like yourself unless you know that others like you. Self-esteem needs the esteem of others to support it.

2. You must ATTRACT your prospect's FAVORABLE ATTENTION to whatever your "sales story" is. The most convincing reasoning in the world will avail nothing unless someone listens. And you must attract *favorable* attention to whatever you are going to say or write or attempt to communicate with your "prospective customer" in any way. How you dress, the sound of your voice, your words of greeting—these may be your "headlines" to attract or repel! *Practice the art of attracting favorable attention!*

3. Then, KEEP 'EM INTERESTED. Half an argument seldom completes a "sale." Your prospect should be made as eager as good, honest advertising can make him to "buy" whatever it is that you are "selling." Only *interesting* reasons will hold his attention, not just "blabbermouth" talk!

4. After arousing your prospect's interest, you must BE CONVINCING. Your prospect must *believe* what you have said. Therefore, you cannot afford to talk or write loosely. Every statement you make must be beyond suspicion. It is far better to be modest and believable than boastful and questionable. Most people avoid arguments, especially if they have nothing to gain even if they "win." Silence is often the loudest answer to anyone whose story is questionable. Try to think of the sculptor who never took a lesson in his life but who produced wonderful statues. When asked how he did such a fine job of carving elephants out of solid blocks of granite he said, "I look at the block and whatever doesn't look like an elephant I chip off. What's left *must* look like an elephant!" In your own thinking, cut out anything that doesn't look and sound convincing—and what's left, in most instances, will be a good piece of "sculpture"—the truth, the real YOU!

5. The fifth function of good advertising is to create an atmosphere to GET ACTION, or agreement. Many advertisers offer something of extra "value" for having acted upon the suggestion made in their advertising. In your personal life it may be only an extra "thank you," or a genuine smile, or a warm goodbye handshake. It costs nothing to make that "extra" effort and it gains much for you personally and socially.

Many people blessed with good minds are handicapped by poor or "average" personalities. They are doomed to remain in the category of the mediocre—simply because they have not been able to create a demand for what they are, what they know, and what they MAY become! In fact, subconsciously they do the things that drive possible "customers" away. Others with no greater mental ability rise to the top simply because they are able to market what skills they possess.

A college professor once divided everything in this world into three classifications:

- The G.A., or General Average,
  which totals 70 percent
- The B.A., or Below Average,
  which amounts to 15 percent

- The A.A., or Above Average,
  which makes up the other 15 percent

This ratio, he explained, included practically everything: people, climate, food, mountains, buildings, manufactured products, books, discoveries, or whatever else you could think of.

Seventy percent of the people in the world, he said, are of average intelligence. They dress alike, think alike, look alike, act alike, ARE alike. There are so many in this group it is difficult indeed to remember anything special about any of them. We quickly forget their names, their faces, their conversation, their work, everything about them. They are the "John and Jane Doe's" of the world, in every phase of life. They like the same books, plays, movies, food, pictures, and each other. They agree on what they dislike. They are the "lost souls" of mankind who never have amounted to much and probably never will.

What about the other 30 percent? As the professor said, half this group, or 15 percent of the total, is Below Average. This percentage applies to countries, scenery, cities, food, manufactured products, paintings, designs, PEOPLE—to anything in fact. Yes, 15 percent of everything is hardly worth a second glance, a second consideration, and—except under extreme circumstances—seldom receives more than its due.

Most important, so far as YOU are concerned, is the 15 percent in the A.A. (Above Average) class. This, as my professor friend explained, includes the people and things that stand out from the crowd. People who make an indelible impression on others by the way they think, talk, walk, dress, write, behave, or generally conduct themselves in their everyday activities. People who, consciously or subconsciously, please, charm, impress favorably. They are the beautiful people. The leaders. They are admired, remembered, perhaps envied, wherever they go, whatever they do. In their business and social lives they make their mark.

Can anyone join this group—this Above Average group? A few belong naturally. But most people must strive to achieve it. How? Let me illustrate. An elderly man was standing on the corner of Fifth Avenue and 57th Street in New York City with a violin case under his arm. A young man approached him and asked how he could get to Carnegie Hall. "It's easy," responded the old man, "practice, *practice,* PRACTICE!"

The aim of this book is to encourage you to practice, *practice,* PRACTICE the qualities that are in demand and appreciated by others and to practice, *practice,* PRACTICE eliminating the qualities that condemn us to mediocrity— to being "just another John or Jane Doe." All this, I believe, will be more quickly understood if presented as methods of "personal advertising." Instead of ideas on advertising a brand of soap, or packaged food, clothing, or any other merchandise, you will find here some thoughts and ideas that will make YOU more acceptable, more easily marketable, more valuable, and more profitable to the "buyer."

Begin now, by advertising YOURSELF TO YOURSELF! Do this and gradually you will make good the slogan "It Pays To Advertise." You'll do it by following basic and proven successful advertising principles. This book does not promise miracles. If one does occur in your life in the form of dramatic improvement, give credit where it is due—to yourself and to your Creator. Remember that the most worthwhile personal attributes must be acquired. Common sense cannot be pounded, hounded, or frightened into you.

And so, as with any ambition, to achieve it, to become a more successful doctor, husband, wife, friend, employee, employer, or whatever one hopes to become, one must "practice, *practice*, PRACTICE!"

Most of this practice revolves around our relationships with human beings and their reactions to *how we look, talk, act, dress, and* REACT TO THEM. As an old-time advertising man, I (irreverently, perhaps) place people in the category of a product for sale in a retail store, of an idea being offered for adoption, or of *any* other commodity being offered to the rest of the world at a price that pays the purveyor a profit and satisfies the purchaser.

I hope I may be forgiven for this seemingly sacrilegious comparison, but what we have to "sell" to other people is what we promise to prospective "buyers" for their money, their love, their friendship, their loyalty, their services, their merchandise, or whatever it is that they have and that we would like to acquire.

When YOU are the "merchandise," idea, or whatever

19

it is that you have to "sell" to reach the Carnegie Hall of your objective, you must practice, *practice,* PRACTICE. One of the best forms of practice is to write, *write,* WRITE. Another, of course, is to read, *read,* READ. And still another is talk, *talk,* TALK. But whether you write, read, or talk, remember you are PRACTICING and, therefore, you must constantly be *improving.* Your mind is like any muscle in your body. It improves with exercise. It deteriorates with laziness. If you set up a schedule to write one letter or one paragraph a day or a week, or read one or two chapters of a book, or even think of what you are going to say when next you meet a "listener"—and then DO it, you will find it easier and easier and easier to do it whenever it seems to be good personal advertising! To be silent is to mail blank sheets of paper to your sweetheart when you really mean to send a love letter.

Change is not easy. It will take some time and a lot of effort; many times you will be discouraged and tempted to give up; you will need encouragement—most of which will have to come from your inner self. Your secret, silent motto from this moment on should be "It Pays To Advertise, and I CAN Do It!"

So, with my sincere best wishes, I hope you will enjoy what follows and that it will help you to reach the stage of success YOU are striving for—YOUR own special "Carnegie Hall"!

2 Know Your "Merchandise"

The very first principle of successful advertising is to know your merchandise and to find in that merchandise some unusual quality that people want. Therefore, you must begin to advertise yourself by knowing yourself, by being able to "merchandise" yourself. If you cannot recognize and capitalize on your good qualities you will be defeated by your average or ordinary qualities. So, the first principle of advertising yourself is definitely *to know yourself*.

Be a tough critic of YOU! Only after you have "sold" your present assets and your potential to yourself can you offer them to others. Keep your personal advertising honest, sincere, dependable, and backed by a moral "money-back" guarantee.

What is true of a product or idea is true of YOU. What are the "weak" spots in your makeup? How can you profit most from your marketable qualities and avoid being hurt by your "weaknesses"? *The right kind of advertising will do it!*

If you think you have no more than average talent you are UNFAIR to yourself. If you are haunted by the thought you did not graduate from a college, or even a high school, if you are embarrassed because your clothes are not expensive, or that you have a limited vocabulary, forget it! These are the flimsiest reasons for surrendering your chances of success. Read the lives of others who reached the top despite these "handicaps."

I, for one, only completed grade school. Times were hard, and even though I was rather lazy I had to start work at an early age. In later years I realized the importance of *knowledge* and envied those who did go through high school and college, so I made up my mind to do something about it. I started reading Dickens, Mark Twain, Shakespeare, and the Holy Bible, which really fascinated me. Bartlett's *Familiar Quotations* was my favorite reference book. Next came the dictionary. Every time I came across a word I did not understand I asked Mr. Webster what it meant! Soon I learned that if you grab a little knowledge here and there you soon acquire enough to put to practical use.

Accept your limitations—but don't knock yourself. If you don't talk about how terrible you are, a lot of people may evaluate you as a fine and capable person. You may be sure of this: no one will ever value you higher than you value yourself.

The golden opportunity for success and better living results from the right kind of advertising of the good qualities of your personality. It opens the door to the minds of others so they enjoy being with you, and are happy to work with you and for you. *Your* personality is the "merchandise" YOU have to "sell" to others to make yourself a success. Make the most of it. A first step toward this is to realize that you, and you alone, can act today as the molder of *the future you.* Look in a mirror. See yourself as others see you! Analyze yourself just as you would a piece of merchandise.

Just as the advertising of products or services must have certain qualifications, so must your advertising of yourself have the same qualifications.

How do others judge you? Certain characteristics seem to "show" prominently and unmistakably on your forehead, your cheeks, your hands, in your eyes, and in your gestures. If you are a constant "frowner," telltale lines will reveal it in your face, but if you smile easily other telltale lines, equally unmistakable, will show. To make the most of a welcome disposition try to analyze your own—and see what kind of advertising YOU have been doing for YOURSELF!

Remember that *every time you speak* you make your listeners feel comfortable or uncomfortable, cooperative or antagonistic. Do you "overact" when you should be modest? Are you a "good sport" in whatever situation you find yourself?

Solicit the help of others. Some of them have been

23

down the road ahead of you and know the rough and smooth places from experience. They're usually quite pleased when asked to give a hand. When they say "Call on me if you get stuck," take them up on it. Do call on them—as often as you need advice or help. It breeds respect and friendship. A prospect or a customer who has been around a long time can wise you up fast if approached the right way. A plain and honest admission that you need to know something will usually bring out sincere interest. Seek information or explanations. *Questions flatter the ego and give you a chance to find out what your prospect really knows and feels.*

When we were tiny children, it seemed to me that the word we most frequently heard was "DON'T." "Don't do this. Don't touch that. Don't, *don't,* DON'T." Because of these sharp warnings we had to learn many things through experiencing them, painful as some of them were.

We learned that fire was hot, that ice was cold, that falling down stairs could hurt us, that the possibilities of childhood disaster were many, and we profited by our personal experiences. But discovering every possible dangerous consequence of our decisions all by ourselves is time consuming, painful, expensive, and sometimes impossible. Therefore, whenever the experiences of others are available, take advantage of them. Listen carefully to those who have arrived through their own series of trials and errors, and avoid most of them by getting to know what NOT to do! Ideally, we should be able to learn that fire is hot without getting burned ourselves.

24

My first lesson in advertising came before I was a week old. Whenever I was hungry, sleepy, in pain, or merely uncomfortable, I advertised as loudly as my infant lungs would permit—until relief arrived! Thus, even before I could read, write, or speak, I found that while cooing and laughing were "headlines" that made me attractive, screaming and screeching usually brought the results I needed to prevent my going down the drain, starving, freezing, or whatever other real or imaginary ills troubled me. That was how I learned that attracting attention was one of the first requisites for getting results.

If you are going through life wondering what's wrong with you, STOP WONDERING! You KNOW! If you really don't, or won't admit it, this book might serve to remind you and, I hope, point you in the right direction to your best chance for success.

It is not what you know, or *think* you know, that counts, it is WHAT YOU DO. You may know all about your product, yourself, but unless you can use that knowledge effectively to ATTRACT FAVORABLE ATTENTION, KEEP 'EM INTERESTED, BE CONVINCING, and GET ACTION from your prospect, It Is of no value to you in advertising yourself!

25

3 Seven Deadly Advertising Mistakes

In the April 29, 1952, issue of the *New York Times* a full-page advertisement for my advertising agency appeared, bearing the headline "Seven Deadly Advertising Mistakes." While it may seem at first glance to be violently negative in its appeal, the ad brought in requests for more than 10,000 copies of its contents in booklet form, from all over the world, not only from folks engaged in the advertising field but from students, college professors, and others not remotely connected with the advertising business.

My conclusion then was that by pointing out and analyzing MISTAKES in advertising that, if agreed to, could then be AVOIDED, one's advertising could be improved.

Now, in this book, which attempts to employ advertising as a means of self-promotion, I cannot help starting by pointing out the *seven deadly* PERSONAL *mistakes* you may be making that hurt your chances for success!

1. The first deadly advertising mistake was to give the reader a reason for *not* reading an ad! Or for *not* paying any attention to your mailing or broadcast message. The first mistake YOU can make is to offer your "prospect" a quick excuse for *not* being interested in you or in whatever you are offering. You may fail to give your prospect an incentive to be interested. Your general appearance may be too dull, too blatant, too obviously a selfish attempt to sell. The basis of all successful advertising is that it PROMISES something, a bargain, health, wealth, love, or acclaim. Test your approach. Does it PROMISE anything as a reward for listening? Is your approach appealing?

When my office was on Madison Avenue in New York a fresh young advertising writer came to me looking for a job. I didn't think much of him but he offered to bet me $10 that he could write a full page newspaper ad, solid type, and that I would read every word of it. That got my attention! To convince me, he showed me only the headline. It read:

"This Page Is All About Maxwell Sackheim."

I not only paid him the $10 bet, but I gave him the job. How could I do anything else?—particularly when he explained that under the headline he would show a recent photograph of my favorite person.

Beware of Deadly Mistake No. 1: NEVER GIVE YOUR PROSPECT A CHANCE TO SAY NO BEFORE YOU EVEN GET STARTED!

2. The second deadly advertising mistake is using headlines that are *dead* lines, that "whisper sweet nothings;" headlines that do not arouse the slightest interest. In fact, they act as "stoppers" from wanting to know more about the product. The second mistake YOU can make is to use opening remarks that mean absolutely nothing to your prospect. People are busy, their time is limited, their interests usually narrow; if you don't impress them as an interesting person, if you don't "hit them between the eyes," you will get only a passing glance. Your prospect won't get excited unless what YOU are offering is important. The reason so many people fail is that they take too much for granted, they think the public "owes" them a "reading." In short, they promise nothing!

Beware of Deadly Mistake No. 2: DO NOT "WHISPER SWEET NOTHINGS" THAT PROMISE NOTHING.

3. The third deadly advertising mistake is "using pictures that do not talk." People, like ads, are always in competition. If your appearance does not convey something out of the ordinary to your prospect, then, figuratively, you are a "picture that does not talk." When people meet you, they judge you by two things—how you look and what you say.

Your appearance should convey what you wish to appear to be: businesslike, vivacious, intelligent, appealing, or whatever type of person you wish to be. And if what you say matches how you look, your advertising is good. Does what you say convey a promise? Does it enlighten or entertain? Are you saying it just because it is "attractive" or "cute"? Is it closely related to your theme? A "picture must do a job" to earn its value! There must be a *valid* reason for its use. A "picture" (how you look and what you say) should be a *plus,* not a minus!

Beware of Deadly Mistake No. 3: DO NOT BE A "PICTURE THAT DOES NOT TALK"!

4. The fourth deadly advertising mistake is the "curse of cleverness." Clever plays on words and attempts to be funny usually fall flat, except when an experienced professional funny man uses them in a stage presentation. The fourth mistake YOU can make is to attempt to be "clever" or a "smart aleck." The curse of cleverness is represented by the "funny guy" whose jokes are so worn with use that he's uninteresting and boring to most people. People who can make others laugh have a wonderful talent, particularly when they can dispense their humor in a professional manner and in wholesale quantities. But amateurs should beware of injury from this double-edged sword! Humor certainly has its place, but that may not be in any attempt to sell "merchandise." Bob Hope and Jack Benny sold a lot of Jell-O and other products with their humor, but there are very, very few Bob Hopes and Jack Bennys in the advertising or social world.

Beware of Deadly Mistake No. 4: DON'T TRY TO BE CLEVER; BEWARE OF THE CURSE OF CLEVERNESS.

5. The fifth deadly advertising mistake is to "go around Robin Hood's barn." When a thought must reach the brain through a series of intricate mental switches, gears, springs, and motors, it's a poor conductor of an idea. The fifth deadly mistake YOU could be making is telling a prospective customer a long-winded story that you might have told in a couple of sentences. Don't be like the attorney who jokes, "Why use twenty words when fifty-eight will do?" In conversation or written advertisements the longest way around is hardly ever the shortest way home. I call it "going around Robin Hood's barn." Coca-Cola doesn't do it. Neither does Ivory Soap. I'm sure you get the point. Undoubtedly *your customer* will listen intently to stories or speeches that could be of value, but when your "customer" begins to yearn for the finish of a sentence, the jig is up. The brain will absorb only what the seat will tolerate. So keep your "customer's" interest.

Beware of Deadly Mistake No. 5: AVOID LONG-WINDED STORIES; DON'T GO AROUND ROBIN HOOD'S BARN TO GET TO YOUR POINT.

6. The sixth deadly advertising mistake is to "leave 'em dangling." If your prospect is interested and convinced by your "sales talk," why risk a forgetting-time instead of providing a "getting-time." The sixth deadly mistake YOU could be making is losing your prospect because of inertia. People intend to do certain things, intend to buy certain products, but they forget, neglect to follow through, change their minds, or become disinterested if you let them "dangle" instead of promising them something. Give your prospect the "GO BUY" instead of the "go-by"!

31

Prospective customers can be "left dangling" if an advertiser fails to say goodbye meaningfully. "Sales" talk should be continued, rather than terminated, with a request for an order or for an opportunity to meet again, or *some* specific admission on the part of the listener or reader, for another appointment to "supply more information" if the prospect is really interested.

Beware of Deadly Mistake No. 6: DON'T "LEAVE 'EM DANGLING" AFTER YOU'VE SOLD 'EM!

7. The seventh deadly advertising mistake is to "use yackety-yak copy." In conversation, this simply means talk, talk, talk, endless talk. It's just noise in their ears. It's turning them off. They'll soon find a way to end the barrage on their eardrums. Courtesy may give the incessant talker an "audience" but your prospect will soon tire of hearing you. The seventh deadly mistake YOU could be making is talking too much. Your self-advertising must be believable. Stop patting yourself on the back. Stop talking just for the sake of hearing your own voice. If you have anything worthwhile to say, SAY IT, but don't insult your prospect's intelligence by trying to overtalk or doubletalk. *You* are what should be bought. When your words clutter up whatever impression you may want to create, cut them out!

Beware of Deadly Mistake No. 7: DON'T USE "YACKETY-YAK" TALK; DON'T TALK TOO MUCH.

The point of analyzing these seven deadly advertising mistakes is to emphasize them so that YOU can avoid them.

32

Whatever your business, profession, or occupation, you will benefit by avoiding them. Your spoken and written words will attract more favorable *attention*. You will be able to create more *interest* in what you are attempting to "sell." You will be more *convincing,* and you will induce more people to *act* upon your "advertising"!

Advertising does not command attention merely *because* it is advertising. Unless the reader is given a substantial *reason* for reading an ad he will give it no more than a passing glance. "Just another ad" is just another advertising tragedy.

It is astonishing how many advertising approaches FAIL to give the public a single *incentive* to heed them. Still worse, many ads actually kill interest in the product promoted at the very first glance. This is even more true of personalities than it is of any other type of "product"!

4 Attract Favorable Attention

To advertise yourself successfully you must *attract attention* that is *favorable,* not outlandish. It should not be so out of character that it attracts attention to *itself* rather than to the *product.* (And remember, YOU are now the product!)

In your personal life *you* as a "product" can attract attention by the way you dress, by the way you comb your hair, by the tone of your voice, by the time you spend talking instead of listening, by noticeable habitual gestures. Some people even attract attention by their complete *lack* of any obvious attempt to do so!

You advertise yourself in all forms of communication—the telephone, letter writing, courtesies or discourtesies shown to others under various conditions, and in many other ways—as you will readily admit if you are fully observant of other people AND yourself!

As a self-advertiser the first thing your "prospective customer" notices about you is the "headline" of your "ad"—your appearance! To attract attention does not require that you must wear hand-tailored, expensive, or wildly colored, fancy clothes. It does mean neatness, cleanliness, courtesy, and not being too aggressive. It does not mean excessive use of powder and perfume, a flower-decorated lapel or hairdo. It does mean good old-fashioned bathtub cleanliness.

Men must respect the "prospective customer" by appearing with hair neatly brushed, nails free from grime. Women should realize that it is just as easy to overdress by wearing too little as by wearing too much. Overexposure of breasts and legs in revealing outfits should be avoided, as should heavy makeup that overemphasizes eyebrows, lips, and cheeks. For both men and women, a more natural, conservative look is better.

A flashy appearance is an artificial headline—a "false alarm" calling attention to those very peculiarities of your personality that you wish to deemphasize instead of directing the prospect's attention to what is being offered!

To attract *favorable* attention is the purpose of making the right impression upon your "prospect." It is far better to *underplay* your attractiveness, your beauty, your sense of humor, your intelligence, your skill, than to *overplay* it.

There are many keys to your ability to attract or reject attention. Your facial expression and gestures reveal your feelings, your attitudes. The clenched fist, the raised eyebrow, the bowed head, the open arms, the extended

36

hand, the drooping mouth, the compressed lips, the "set" jaw, the shrugged shoulder; these and other telltale signals indicate what you are thinking even before you say a word. You may subconsciously reveal your likes or dislikes at first sight.

To wave your arms wildly while discussing a subject is both distracting and an affront to your listener's intelligence. Even worse, it's a demonstration of your own inability to make yourself understood without the use of motions. This habit of using the arms, the face, the hands, the legs, the body to project one's meaning may have been essential in the days of silent movies. But few performers of those days survived with the advent of talkies and television! The better your ideas are and the more convincing your story, the less need there is for you to pound the table when talking. A soft voice, even a whisper, can frequently speak louder than a shout. You may be forced to use your hands when describing a "circular" stair case—but not dramatically.

So the headline of *your ad for yourself* is YOUR AP-PEARANCE. To destroy that, or exaggerate it, is to force the "reader" or "listener" or whoever may be the object of your solicitation through any medium of communication (for an order, a position, a favor or merely for an agreement with your thinking) to discount or even ignore whatever appeal may follow that "headline."

People do not act out of mere curiosity. People will not believe what you say just because you say it. People will not respond to your advertising unless there is ample incentive for them to do so. Your first job in advertising yourself is to *attract attention—favorable attention.* Unless this is accomplished all else in your "advertisement" is immaterial.

The line between honesty in attracting others and complete sincerity may be very thin, but you as an "advertising expert" may be trying to bring yourself and the "purchaser" together too abruptly if your efforts are too obvious. Others are courting your prospect too. As my friend John Caples, a New York advertising executive, said in his book *Tested Advertising Methods,* "There is no element in an advertisement more important than the reason, or reasons, you give for people to favor you and your ideas as you meet and talk to them." Even if you stammer and stutter while you say things worth hearing, it will "sell" your ideas much better than "smooth" talk that says nothing or "too much"!

Now let me illustrate what I mean by "favorable attention." One of my first jobs was as a delivery boy for an advertising company in Chicago, back in the early 1900s. One snowy day, I was standing at a window watching some boys playing tag in the snow. As I watched them I got an idea. I went out to the side of the building where the president's office was located, where the snow was untrampled. Then in the new fallen snow I tramped out the initials of our company, and it made an impressive sign. The president of the company saw me tramping out the sign and when I came back into the building he called me into his office and praised my "ingenuity" and gave me a

50¢ raise, from $3.00 to $3.50 a week! (That was a big raise in those days.) You see, this idea had attracted his favorable attention. The principle remains now as then: attract the favorable attention of those who can advance you in your personal, social, or business life.

One of the lessons I learned while an office and errand boy with a large advertising agency was to generate enthusiasm in everything I did. When I began as an errand boy, shuffling along was part of my makeup, and it was evident in the way I performed my work, to the point where it seemed I was "goldbricking" even when carrying papers from one desk to another—only ten feet away! One day one of the advertising copywriters called me into his office and spoke rather sharply.

"Why do you shuffle along when you walk around the office?" he said. "You make everyone think you are lazy, and that's no way to get ahead. Why don't you try speeding up when you walk? It will look a lot better—it will make everyone think you are ambitious instead of thinking you are lazy—and you will find yourself in an entirely new world of enthusiasm and ambition.

"People judge you by your own opinion of yourself! If you are slow-pokey, indifferent in your daily job, everybody may feel sorry for you but they will not help you. Why not try the 'busy-bee' way to walk and talk and work? Start asking questions about our work, or about anything, and before you realize it someone will be asking you questions—because they will think you know the answers."

After that pep talk I learned to walk fast, think fast, ask

39

questions fast, answer them fast—and earn a fast buck! Advertise your brightness and many other fine qualities by being alive and alert instead of weary, dopey, and dull! There is always a new goal to be reached, a new problem to be solved; it should keep you thinking about where you are, where you want to go—and about others, what they want and need, how to reach them. Advertising stretches you, makes you use all of your abilities and develop new ones.

Don't sell yourself short, and don't let anyone else do it! You are the most precious, the most valuable, the most usable commodity you own. So keep in mind always the thought of who you really are and how important you are.

How to determine the proper and most effective approach to the ideal personality "headline" is subject to analysis of yourself and others, of those who have succeeded and of those who have failed. This applies to men as well as to women, to business people, actors, professionals—even gamblers!

When I was in New York I used the C.O.D. technique to sell Little Leather Library books by mail. The headline was "Send No Money." This headline plus the price—"All 30 of These Classics for Only $2.98"—attracted attention. I found it much easier to sell C.O.D. than to obtain cash in advance. I believe it was the first time books were ever sold by mail on this basis. Eventually this led to the idea for the Book-of-the-Month Club. This same idea can apply to *you*—sell your prospect before you expect anything in advance.

There have been many versions of how the Book-of-the-Month Club was started, but the basic idea was simple. We attracted attention with the idea of supervised selection and automatic shipment unless a rejection card was returned, and this idea was favorably accepted by book lovers, publishers, authors.

And so it is with products and PEOPLE. Some are wisely advertised and some are almost laughed at by the public, if not audibly, silently by the public's weapon—*not to buy* what is offered.

What is true of a product or idea is true of YOU. What do you have to offer others? What are the "weak" spots in your makeup? How can you profit most by your marketable qualities and avoid being hurt by your "weak spots"? The right kind of advertising will do it!

When I was a young man my first thought was always "How can I attract favorable attention to what I have to offer?" I remember when I went to work in the advertising department at Sears, Roebuck in 1913; it was like working in a large advertising agency. There were about fifty departments in the company. Some departments required ads in farm publications, others in women's magazines, sporting publications, or in the religious press. Still others needed help in preparing catalog pages or assistance in direct-mail programs, while some needed all three—ads, catalog pages, and direct mail. No one told me to do it, but I worked "all over the lot."

A day or two after I went to work there I determined to adopt a "promotion policy" of my own and make each

41

department "my client." I began to furiously write memos to everybody in the organization I thought would be interested. I wasted no time in attempting to put myself "on the map." The advertising manager had written me a memo. "Why not reply in kind? not with one memo but with many," I asked myself. Accordingly a veritable stream of memoranda, all duly signed "Sackheim," began to land on the manager's desk—containing what I believed to be helpful ideas and suggestions.

I broached my idea to him for a Sears, Roebuck Advertising Club to be made up of the advertising managers, copywriters, and any others interested, from any of the fifty or more departments. He approved the idea, and I sent a memo to all catalog-copy men asking what they thought of a cooperative clearinghouse for catalog-copy men in the various departments with the object of exchanging ideas. Anyone can "self-promote" a career, even in an establishment as large as Sears. The habit of writing memos—and making suggestions—becomes a challenge to one's own thinking. And it may result in big ideas and big jobs.

In my eagerness to get ahead I continued to direct a stream of memos with suggestions of all kinds—most of which were turned down. But this made me try even harder. I wrote even more memos and put more effort into them. It was my way of advertising myself, of making my presence and my work known. As a result I became Assistant Advertising Manager for Sears, Roebuck Co. at the age of 23. Anyone in any line of business, industry or profession can ADVERTISE himself by attracting favorable attention to himself!

42

During World War II my advertising training came to the rescue of the firm I then headed. I offered our services to the government in any capacity it could use them. To accomplish this I again adopted a basic advertising principle: *attract attention*. Instead of sending letters, I directed long telegrams to everyone in Washington I thought would be interested in our equipment and experience, and followed these telegrams with phone calls and personal visits. I knew nothing about manufacturing but was able to get our name on the list of various procurement divisions so we could bid on some of the things the government needed.

When we were asked if we could do certain jobs we said "Yes, if we have additional equipment." So they lent us the money for the equipment and we did the work. When we knew absolutely nothing about a certain type of job, we employed people who did know! It was a continuous learning process, involving new requirements, new methods, new equipment. But we did the job.

I'm sure we never could have gotten anywhere in our war work if not for the advertising training that taught me to learn the merchandise, *attract favorable attention, stimulate interest, carry conviction*, and *induce action*. These basic principles can be applied to almost anything anyone wants. Certainly you cannot interest anyone in anything without first attracting attention; you cannot convince anyone without gaining interest; and unless you get action it is useless to attract attention, gain interest, or convince.

The person reading or listening to your story must be attracted quickly, ideally with a very few words, by an attention grabber your prospect can't resist.

43

Every time you speak you advertise yourself for better or worse. By the way, how good a listener are you? A good salesman sells by listening as well as by talking. Do you make your prospects feel comfortable by your attitude, speech, and actions? Do you use a soft voice even when it's necessary to be tough? As the Bible says, "A soft voice turneth away wrath." Nearly everything about you advertises you—the lettering on your door, the letters you write and the ones you don't write, the appearance of your office, the way your telephone is answered, the way you remember or forget names and faces. Do you take yourself too seriously? Or do you have a sense of humor? Do you have a hidden contempt for the other people and their opinions? Do you acknowledge an introduction in a sincere manner? Do you carry a chip on your shoulder that may advertise an inferiority complex? Do you give orders and instructions so they are clearly understood or are people in a fog after you tell them what you want? There are countless ways to advertise successfully. You know them as well as, or better than, any advertising man. Courtesy is advertising. Promptness is advertising. Tolerance is advertising. You can advertise favorably even when you must say no, if you say it graciously. These things cost nothing but they are the ingredients of successful, personal advertising.

To attract attention you must shake people out of their complacency. We hate to change our minds, our habits, our routines. It takes tons of persuasion to get us to do or think what we *want* to do or think, to say nothing of the effort involved in shifting our mental gears to accommodate you. *The best way to* ATTRACT FAVORABLE ATTENTION *is to direct your appeal to your prospect's interest—not* YOURS!

Checklist for Attracting Favorable Attention

1. Your "headline" is your appearance, the first sentence of your letter or talk, your facial expression, your gestures.
2. Be honest in everything you say or write.
3. Take pride in yourself.
4. Show interest and concern for other people.
5. Be enthusiastic—but not overly so—in expressing your ideas and opinions.

5 Keep'Em Interested

The key to interesting anyone in any thought you may have lies in the art of proper communication! Any attempt to deliver a message in any form is like talking to the four winds unless it is received. So, after attracting attention make sure your message is heard, read, seen, UNDERSTOOD!

No matter what you say or how you say it, no matter how well or how poorly you dress, regardless of what method you may use for attracting attention, your advertising of yourself doesn't do the job for you, doesn't "sell" you or your ideas to your "prospect," unless you *interest* those whose *attention* you have attracted! You must *interest* them in what you have to offer—your personality, your knowledge, your ability, your future value to them—or whatever it is that you are attempting to "sell." You must hold attention by what you say, and how you say it—whether in writing, speech, sign language, or however you convey your message. It is not what you think you can do for your prospective "customer" that counts; it is what your prospective "customer" thinks you can do for him! You are the most interesting subject to YOU and your potential customers are most interested in themselves, so—to keep their interest—relate to what is important to your customer.

You must assume that everyone is equipped with a remote-control gadget like those used with television sets. You press a button to silence the commercial or change the station. Our personal gadget is *indifference* and *inertia*. We glance at headlines and pictures with one eye, we listen with half an ear, we meet people and forget their names at once, if we get them at all. We read books and see plays, and we're bored unless there is something very special about them. We go through life with our minds usually only half turned on. Our attitude, generally, about nearly everything is "so what?" and that hurdle must be taken at every step in the process of getting people to act. To induce anyone to drop everything else in order to pay attention to you, whether you write, speak, or act, you must hang on to your audience by keeping them interested. Don't trifle with their demand for some benefit they must receive from paying attention to you—if only for a few minutes of their time and thought or a few pennies of their money.

The most important thing in talking to one or more people is for YOU to have a sincerely friendly feeling. Smile frequently but sincerely. Cultivate a warm understanding

48

and you will smile at the correct time, and when you smile it will be contagious.

The same is true of your handshake. If you convey a sincere liking for whomever you are shaking hands with you will be extending a firm and gracious hand of friendship. Do not give anyone a limp collection of fingers or a grip of steel in which you can crush a hand. Offer a hand that says, as no other greeting can say, "I'm really and truly glad to meet you."

Friendliness begets friendliness. This is profoundly true, and I may add that people in a friendly mood are in a buying mood! A cheerful, sincere greeting calls for a cheerful, sincere response.

In this modern day and age someone produces a product that almost sells itself. It is so obviously desired that very little publicity may be required to induce the public to buy it. Unfortunately this is not so true of people. Individuals seldom have the opportunity to advertise themselves as new inventions that perform unusual services. Most automatic mental responses to personal sales efforts make personal advertising practically useless. The wrong approach to the prospective consumer's problem, the too obvious urge to "buy, buy, buy" instead of the unselfish attitude of "look what this means to you" causes prospective customers to turn a deaf ear and a closed mind to whatever is offered.

Conversation can be, and usually is, so dull that it skips by the "listener's" mind and is almost entirely ignored. Even among the well educated, it is almost frightening how frequently the words "you know" are used. They are an unconscious speech habit that deprives a thought of its real force. If the speaker says "you know," why should he repeat what you know? It is almost an insult to the intelligence of the listener to harp on what "he knows."

It is discouraging, to say the least, to listen to anyone who uses big words merely for the purpose of trying to impress an audience or an individual. If you want to say "dog," say "dog"—it isn't necessary to say "canine." If you really want to appreciate how strenuously some writers and speakers strain to make impressions rather than "converts" read any magazine or newspaper article and underscore the words whose meaning you don't instantly grasp.

It is much easier to be yourself than to imitate others; much easier to convey your thinking with a small vocabulary that is *yours* than a large one that does not always express your own ideas. If you use your own words to describe your feelings, communication becomes clear to your reader or audience, and especially to YOURSELF! The more economical you are with words, the more meaningful your words are, because what you say is fully understood.

Basically, the most important factor in communication, whether written or spoken, is that you do not appear to be hiding behind big words. It is better to be natural! Educated readers understand short words but most people may not understand long words! Even where it is necessary to substitute several short words for one long word, it is usually wise to do so, especially before an average group. When we drag in a lot of unfamiliar words we ourselves sometimes forget just what it was we were trying to say, and the "prospect" never does find out. Short words are easy and pleasant to read and to hear, and their meaning is instantly understood by every listener. The average person stumbles over fancy words. After about two minutes of trying to absorb their meaning his interest wanders and he turns to other thoughts that can be grasped without effort. Why bother trying to unravel someone else's vocabulary?

When there is a communication misunderstanding or breakdown we are quick to blame the other fellow, but before you condemn him ask yourself if you could have been more explicit. Many people know what they *want* to say. But when it's said, it's not clear to them and certainly not to their prospects. Their language actually withholds information essential for easy understanding. And some talk or write to "impress" others.

If you talk too much about yourself, you will find yourself talking to yourself. Try to invite the listener or reader, whom you assume to be a person of intelligence, to join in the conversation. Don't start by telling him something he already knows. Begin by telling him something new.

Your words need to convey a feeling of interest, a glow of friendliness, the assurance of sincerity, and the impression that you believe the message to be of sufficient importance to warrant the attention of those that you want to "sell" it to.

Words should clarify instead of cloud! Even if people do not agree with your meaning, talk and write so there can be no doubt about what you are saying. To put a thought into words that deliver a message clearly has the virtue of making it seem more real, honest, and believable than if you mumble it or surround it with a lot of extra words that smother it.

Some people suggest you should "write as you speak," but you must keep in mind that it is easier to get an idea across in speech than in writing. One reason is that when speaking you can stress some words and pause at some places. In writing, all the words of a sentence are usually printed in equal blackness, separated by the same amount of space. Therefore in writing, your choice of words should take the place of stresses and pauses that can be made in speaking.

As to the length of your "talks": Abraham Lincoln's Gettysburg Address consisted of ten sentences and was spoken in three minutes. On the same platform, the orator of the day was the famous Edward Everett, who had been a U.S. senator, governor of Massachusetts, secretary of state, and minister to Great Britain. He spoke for an hour and fifty-seven minutes. Lincoln's words are immortal—Everett's are forgotten.

A good speech or piece of writing communicates a thought; it conveys a feeling and gives the reader or listener some benefit. It must not be too pompous or hesitant about what it seeks to do, or beneath the intelligence of your audience, or too arrogant for your position.

When a good idea strikes you, make a note of it. You can be critical later. The first draft should be done at once!

Smoothing and polishing can follow later. So write it down at once, even roughly. Writing is a form of rehearsing privately!

Continued writing will clear up your doubts, hazy thinking, vague mental indigestion, and other mental limitations. The more difficult it is for you to write, the more you need to do it. No matter how silly your first attempts may seem to be, keep writing. Each word you write will make you think of another, and each sentence will suggest another, if you write it down.

The more you write the more new ideas you'll create to form more building blocks for new ideas. Don't stop writing when you read your written words and find them dull.

Naturally, whatever you put on paper lacks the inflection of your voice, lacks the expression of your face, and is judged only by the words and thoughts the eyes and mind of the reader behold. Writing is excellent practice in clear thinking, a wonderful experience in advertising yourself, and it can be a great attention getter.

Even letters that express opposite opinions to those generally accepted have a certain effect upon people that spoken words do not carry. Your own reading and ability to judge will profit greatly by your writing. You will learn from your writing how to say yes. Just as important, if not more so, you will learn how to say no gracefully.

I suggest that you write at least one letter a day to a relative, a friend, a newspaper, a magazine, or even to yourself. It will stir your imagination; it will make you want to

53

read more, learn more, think more, write more; and it will give you the gift of self-expression that you will not otherwise have.

For practice, as James T. Mangan said: "Write a letter . . . it's only a few steps to the nearest mail box. Take a little chunk of your heart and spread it over some paper; it goes, oh, such a long way.

"Write a letter to yourself if you can't bring yourself to write to your mother or father, to your sister, brother, sweetheart, loved ones. Are your relatives and friends dear to you? Prove it with a letter! Are they far from you? Bring them near to you with a letter! Give them the same thrill you had when you last received a letter from them. Think of the joy of opening the mailbox and drawing out a warm envelope enriched with old familiar handwriting!

"There's a man in public life you admire, believe in, rave about. Write him a letter of praise, of encouragement. To be 'with him in spirit' is not enough—show your spirit with a letter. We can't all be pioneers, crusaders, presidents—BUT we can help those brave men stay on the track and push through to success if all we ever say is 'Attaboy!' Write an 'Attaboy' letter! And remember, the real letter is the ONE YOU DON'T HAVE TO WRITE!

"The greatest men of all times and all nations have been regular letter writers. Try it, you'll like it. You'll get letters back. You'll get help from unexpected sources. All that you gave in your letters will be returned to you a thousand-fold. For a letter is an investment in bountiful good fortune."

The written word cannot bore the reader—he can stop reading whenever his interest lags. The spoken word is much more difficult to endure if it is dull. The best way to advertise your thoughts is to write them down, then when you are "sold" on them you can feel confident of their appeal to a *listener!* The art of clear communication is the heart of good advertising—and good advertising can be produced by anyone who can *write* interestingly!

Communication often fails because one or both parties are not listening. They may nod and smile, but their ear passages may as well be sealed with concrete for all that is getting through to their brains. Some people are so enamored of their own voice that they can't listen to anyone else. Others have such a short attention span that they soon tire of listening. Still others are too busy planning their next comment to hear anything that is being said to them by anyone!

The easiest form of communication for everyone is talking. Because it is so easy it is much more frequently overdone than underdone. What has already been said cannot be crossed out and "corrected." Therefore, you must THINK BEFORE YOU SPEAK. Practice speaking even when you are alone and even if you say only one sentence at a time. You may be shocked, startled, disgusted, or you may be delighted with your own reaction to your voice and your thinking. Much depends on what you say. It is not necessary for you to be an orator; it is, however, necessary that your words convey some meaning that reflects a thought worth listening to. Even if you must read your words instead of reciting them from memory, they can sound convincing, depending on how sincerely you say them.

As James Maratta wrote: "We make judgments of another person's real meanings from the tone of his voice, not only from his words. When a person says 'get out of here' it is the tone of his voice that conveys whether he is joking or serious."

Above all, in conversation, even if you are sure you are right, avoid argument. If you triumph over the other man and shoot his argument full of holes, you will feel fine. But you will have made him feel inferior. You will have hurt his pride. Remember: "A man convinced against his will, is of the same opinion still."

Let anyone who seems eager to do so beat you in any petty discussion that may arise. It will cost you nothing, and your ultimate reward will be greater health, more friends, longer life, and more prosperity.

As Dale Carnegie said in many of his lectures: "No one likes to feel that he is being sold something. We much prefer to feel that we are buying of our own accord and not being "sold." We like to be consulted about our wishes, our wants, our thoughts. So let the other fellow feel that the idea is his."

A real salesman gives ideas and plans to everyone he thinks can use them to help improve their status in life. He gives his friends and even strangers solutions to their problems whenever he can. The more he gives to others, the better he enjoys life. Be a GIVER and you will discover that the deepest secret of getting is in the giving—and that the more you GIVE the more you will have left in your account!

The art of communication includes not only what you write and say but how you answer the following questions *to yourself!*

- Do you think only of making a sale instead of making a friend? A sale may make a one-time profit for you but a friend may "buy" a hundred times.
- Do you criticize your competition or ignore competitive comparisons? Remember the old saying: "Every knock is a boost."
- Are you specific in making your claims? Remember it is easier to concentrate on one good point than diluting the strength of your claims by scattering them among many "good" points.
- Do you *talk* too much and *listen* too little? Your own conscience and the reaction of your listeners can answer this for you!
- Do you sometimes admit frankly that you have been wrong? Try it. It's a wonderful way to compliment an opponent, win his friendship. And it usually costs you nothing!

Know your product (YOURSELF). Know your market (whoever you are trying to "sell" or "convince"). Then follow the formula that has proved so successful in obtaining traceable results through advertising. Communicate in every way that builds, *builds,* BUILDS up personality!

By all means never stop thinking, and think as wildly and as "crazily" as your mind can reach. If you review almost any line of invention or discovery made during the past century or more you will realize how easily they could have been discouraged.

Practice writing and practice speaking to sell yourself on these two great heaven-sent gifts to "keep 'em interested."

Checklist for Keeping 'Em Interested

1. Say or write what is of interest to your audience.
2. Make yourself understood.
3. Sell yourself by listening.
4. Be courteous, prompt, and tolerant in advertising yourself.
5. Be sincere and friendly.
6. Break the "you know" habit.
7. Use simple language anyone can understand.
8. Be yourself. Don't imitate.
9. When you get an idea, write it down. Be critical later.
10. Write at least one letter a day.
11. Use your voice, but give the other person an opportunity to use his, too.
12. Practice speaking alone.
13. Avoid arguments. Let the other person "win."
14. Be a "giver."

58

6 Be Convincing

The fourth step in successful advertising aims definitely to *convince* the prospect —and *conviction depends upon believability*. No matter what you say, if it isn't believed you've lost the sale. Believability is born of sincerity. Even if exaggeration or outright dishonesty does fool "some people some of the time," the graveyard of hopes is filled with examples of products, ideas, and services that failed to make good their promoter's false promises. On the other hand, the history of commercial advertising is filled with examples of honestly promoted products that rose to the top in spite of "handicaps" that, if not openly exposed to the public in advance and sometimes even exploited, would have killed them as far as public acceptance was concerned.

Every advertising man remembers the advertising of

Volkswagen that capitalized on the small size, "ugly shape," and other "features" of the car. By its obvious sincerity the advertising created a certain pride of acceptance, and even a challenge, to ownership! The same is true of people. The blind, the lame, the handicapped—if their virtues are honestly presented, and believed by their "prospects"—can "sell" whatever they are offering. Sometimes these handicaps prove to be unintentional "sales helps"!

Remember the story of the beggar whose sign read "I Am Blind." His tin cup was fairly well filled every day, but when his appeal was changed to "It Is Spring—And I Am Blind" his collections more than doubled!

Keep your advertising consistently honest, sincere, dependable, and accompanied by a moral "money-back" guarantee. Every "claim" you make should be accompanied by some assurance that if you have unintentionally led someone to believe other than the honest truth you will somehow gladly correct your error.

Many, many years ago John Wanamaker built the largest department store in the United States, at the time, simply by telling the truth. If his buyers made a mistake in their selection of an item he said so in his ads, apologized to the public, and offered the "mistake" at a price that made it a real bargain. The same is true of every legitimate merchant or salesman and is applicable to YOU as your "product." If you are wrong, admit it frankly; don't try to lie yourself out of a jam—and, of course, make every effort to avoid lying yourself *into* one! Candor, honesty, decency build not only sales and customers but reputations as well.

The most important single quality a good advertisement must posses is the desire and the ability of the advertiser to be completely honest. When a *human* advertisement exaggerates or deliberately misrepresents whatever he is attempting to "sell"—whether it is his services, his companionship, his skill—he knows when he is attempting to deceive his "customer"! To be completely honest as an advertiser of *yourself* you must feel, think, and react to your appearance, your statements, your whole demeanor as you hope your prospect will. Truth in salesmanship *of your personality* is even more important to YOU than truth in selling any other commodity you are about to advertise.

You can be your own best ally—or your own worst enemy—depending on how you face facts. It is not enough to read only with your eyes or listen only with your ears, you must definitely and consciously wish to know the WHOLE ANSWER.

All the eloquence in the world will not make up for a lack of integrity. To make people like you, you must inspire confidence. They may not agree with your ideas, but they must respect your belief in those ideas. What you are speaks more loudly than what you say. Honesty, sincerity, integrity, modesty, and unselfishness affect an audience deeply. People much prefer a clumsy speaker who radiates honesty to a polished orator who is simply trying to impress. Convince YOURSELF of your worth and you will find it much easier to convince others.

And so in life, the best way to *advertise* yourself convincingly is to be YOURSELF convincing. If you are, no pros-

61

pect will ever be disappointed with what he receives when he compares it to what he was promised, and no "customer" will have to change his original opinion of your value to him.

To convince people, whatever you are offering must revolve around some basic human want. There must be a good and sufficient reason why you think it is better than what your competitor is offering. Surely YOU know something about YOU that your prospect cannot possibly know. Certainly you know things about your product, or service, that you rate very highly and that can always be the "clincher" in your personal sales argument!

Who you are, what you are, what you know, or what you can do becomes important only after your prospect is convinced that you are telling him the truth and that the truth can really help him. So keep on explaining what you can do for him. Don't dwell on your reputation, your past achievements, your abilities. Your past accomplishments may be a comfort to you, but they cannot help your "prospect" unless they are translated into his needs. Your prospect must be made to feel that he is the one who will benefit the most, get the best of the bargain, win all or most of the advantages. Make him feel that what you are getting out of the transaction is small compared with his gain. Keep suggesting that the whole proposition was designed to benefit him and that what YOU get out of it is a by-product of what he wants and needs most, what will make his life more pleasant. Make him feel that twice as many people want what you have to offer than whatever it is that you are "selling."

One of the greatest troubles with some advertising—and with some people—is exaggeration. You have seen countless ads for "half-price" sales, "1¢" sales, "free" offers, special "discount" deals, "fire" sales, "overstock" sales, and so on—sales described in terms limited only by the imagination of the seller and his estimate of the gullibility of the prospective customer. Sometimes the most effective form of "bragging" is the maximum amount of modesty. Remember always what Abraham Lincoln said: "You may fool all the people some of the time; you can even fool some of the people all the time; but you can't fool all of the people all the time."

I am sure that advertising claiming its subject to be "the best," "the biggest," "the most," and so on convinces you less than advertising that affects you by its modesty and by its logic. So it is in your personal life. To advertise yourself most effectively, speak softly instead of yelling or screaming; and in every aspect of life—your dress, your approach to new acquaintances, your association with fellow employees—it is far better and more impressive to let your honesty convey your knowledge and disposition than flamboyant speech or bragging.

Advertising fails when people pooh-pooh its claims. Advertising pays off when readers cannot deny its sincerity. The same is true of personalities, of YOU.

One of the most effective forms of advertising doesn't

seem to be advertising at all—the *recommendation*. This features praise from users of a product or service—and is far more effective than self-praise. The producer, or distributor, doesn't make claims or brag. He simply quotes what others say—and perhaps even softens some of the "claims" made by previous customers! One of the earliest forms of this type of advertising is the old "before and after" picture story. How can this be applied to your personal advertising? There are many ways: by deliberately slowing up or speeding up your speech; by dressing more, or less, colorfully; by writing more letters, or fewer; by talking louder or softer; by gesturing less.

To advertise yourself successfully you must be honest with yourself and others in appearance, in speech, in writing—to your nearest and dearest ones, to your intimate friends, your business associates, to your prospective "customers."

One of the most effective methods of salesmanship has always been the common or ordinary auction sale where people establish their own price for whatever is put up for sale. Nothing compels them to buy and they can stop bidding whenever they wish. In other words, they set their own price for whatever is being offered for sale. It could be related to an individual if he came to a prospective employer and said, "After I work for you for a while, pay me whatever you think I am worth." This is, of course, what happens when a salesman works on a commission basis.

Very few people are beautiful enough to win beauty contests, but most of us can be convincing if we are well groomed, honest, interesting, alert, kind, and generous. There is no reason to berate ourselves because we lack great beauty or talent. Remember, it is far more effective to be NATURALLY sweet and convincing than to be MADE sweet and convincing.

Another effective way to "sell yourself" is to ask the other person to do a favor—one that gives a feeling of importance. When someone asks, "Will you do something for me?" say "Yes, if I possibly can" at once before you know what you're getting into or how big the favor is. Certain things you can always be confident of, and one is your willingness to serve others. In spite of your doubts and fears, you can keep yourself ready to serve—or show a willingness to do so.

There is a very good rule about a favor. Don't do one unless you can do it without expecting anything in return. Either do a favor freely or admit you are not generous enough to stand the test. When you expect gratitude it changes a blessing into a barter.

You are an imperfect human being living in an imperfect world; but whether your mistakes serve as guideposts to lead you to a better road or whipping posts to which you tie yourself for the sake of senseless suffering depends on your understanding and your willingness to conduct your life in accordance with what you learn as you go along. When nothing can be done to correct a mistake, forget it!

Frequently, quality isn't enough of an incentive to bring customers back again and again, and repeat sales, not *first* sales alone, are the lifeblood of business. Sometimes

65

"convenience" is a great asset (witness the success of shopping centers and the decline of "downtown" streets). In most instances, however, personality, personal relationship, and habit keep customers coming "downtown" or "uptown" or wherever "the store" may be—even a day or night away.

The self-confident advertising expert is often required to make sudden decisions and be responsible for the consequences involved. In this decision-making aspect, whatever objective is most important requires the power, self-reliance, and faith of the top executive in any business. Approach self-confidence as if it were another person but still belonging entirely to you, and regard it as your best friend.

When you come into any "prospect's" presence, it is good salesmanship to try to look like you have just come away from writing up a healthy order. Strike a confident pose. As the old saying goes, "To be successful, look successful!"

Thinking for yourself is one of the best ways to increase your source of self-confidence. Don't accept the opinions of others as right just because the "others" are overwhelming in number. DON'T BE ONE OF THE CROWD. Have enough personal integrity to assure yourself that you may be right. Listen well, but prove it to yourself. When you use another's claim to prove your own superiority you aren't nearly so effective as when you first prove the claim to your own satisfaction. Then the proof you offer the prospect is yours, not someone else's! Try not to "kid yourself."

If you were standing in a long line, waiting for your "turn" to purchase tickets for some famous movie or play, or to gain admission to an "all-star" event, you would surely resent anyone behind you pushing, shoving, or attempting in any other way to get ahead of you. So it should be in your business or social life. You simply cannot afford to waste the years (not minutes or even hours as in the examples above) it might take you to be in as good a position to advance as right NOW. Just keep the "other guy" from pushing or shoving his way ahead of you. Indeed, if there's any pushing or shoving to be done, why not be the aggressor yourself instead of the victim—but do it mentally, not physically. You should constantly use your full brainpower to advance yourself on the theory that the fellow, or even several fellows "ahead" of you may be coasting along, depending on reputations earned years ago but now perhaps out of date. This does not mean bragging, or being loudmouthed, but simply to have the confidence to exercise your ability to express yourself forcefully, positively, and with an aura of authority. When you speak, be prepared to back up your opinions with facts, convincing experiences of your own or someone else's. You need not be objectionable in the sense of forcing your opinion on others. But you must do everything possible to make *yourself believable* and convincing. If later you are proven to have been wrong, your conscience will not hurt, because you will have had ample evidence that your position was right, in the light of experience.

Assume the attitude that anything worth saying is

67

worth proving. Don't depend on your pretty face, sexy fig-ure, good looks, manner of dress, grooming or "gift of gab" to pull you through when you want something your pros-pect won't easily give up.

Try always to place yourself in the other person's shoes. Say to yourself, "How would I feel if I were in his place?" You will save a lot of time and annoyance when the answer comes to you!

You cannot learn to judge people accurately if you don't keep your mind open while giving the other person an opportunity to show who he is and what he can do.

When dealing with people, remember you are dealing with creatures bristling with prejudices motivated by vanity. With such an opponent, criticism is a dangerous spark—a spark that could very well cause an explosion, both physical and mental.

Anyone can criticize, condemn, complain. But it takes character to be understanding. Instead of condemning, try to understand. Never mind what a person is or has done. Decide what you want him to be or do and suggest it to him in a pleasant way. One reason so many parents are ineffec-tive in guiding their children, and employers in controlling the behavior of their employees, is that they criticize a past performance that cannot be erased, avoiding future repeti-tion of the offense.

G. Lynn Sumner, a famous advertising man and once advertising manager of the International Correspondence School, frequently told the story of a correspondence school salesman calling on a coal miner who had inquired about a course in engineering. The salesman was "train-ing" a prospective addition to the sales staff. As the coal miner and the student sat down to talk, the salesman was eloquent in his arguments as to why it would pay the miner to take the course he was interested in. He was so convinc-ing that after about thirty minutes the miner reached into his pocket and brought forth the price of the course, in crumpled, soiled dollar bills. So enthusiastic was the trainee that he could not resist the urge to congratulate the star salesman, but the only way he could do it quickly was to nudge his foot. Immediately thereafter the miner picked up the money he had placed on the table and put it back in his pocket, stating that he was going to "think it over." No amount of urging, no amount of pleading could move him again to put his money on the table. The only thing the salesman and the student could do was to leave. As they were leaving the trainee said to the salesman, "I can't un-derstand it, you had him sold. I was so thrilled that I couldn't resist nudging your foot." In reply the star sales-man said, "You didn't nudge *my* foot: you must've nudged *his* foot, and he thought you were warning him to put his money away."

The moral of the story is that you can unconvince a person much quicker than you can convince him. But even after he is convinced, if you make a false move or statement you can undo everything you have said or done. A sly wink, a false gesture, an insincere word can undo hours of con-vincing, honest sales argument!

You can tell people they are wrong by a look or ges-

69

ture much more quickly than by your words—and still not make them want to agree with you! For, regardless of how you convey your message of disagreement, you have struck a direct blow at their judgment, their self-respect.

When people are wrong, they first secretly admit it to themselves. And if they are handled gently and tactfully, they may then admit it to others, and even take pride in their frankness. But they will stubbornly resist admitting they are wrong if someone else is trying to ram that unpalatable fact down their throats!

When anyone is attacked, he stops believing anything anyone else believes and works twice as hard to defend his position. If he has a sense of personal inferiority, he is driven to emphasize the soundness of what he said. It takes a person in fine balance to look at criticism objectively.

If you are going to prove anything, it is better to say "Well, I thought otherwise, but I may be wrong. Let's examine the facts." Nobody will ever object to your saying "I may be wrong." That will stop all argument. It may make him admit that he might be wrong too.

When you can "sell" the total stranger the picture you want him to have of you, you have proved that you are a "salesman"! You have been believable and convincing.

The most important "merchandise" you have to sell is YOU! You cannot possibly accomplish ANY "sale" unless you *know your "merchandise"*; you cannot possibly create a "market" for YOU unless you *attract favorable attention* to yourself; you MUST *hold the interest* of your prospective "customer"; you must *convince* him that your price is a

70

bargain for what he is getting—and finally you MUST *induce him to act* upon your sales presentation. Let's now see what can help you to induce ACTION—without which practically all our other "advertising" efforts may be wasted.

Checklist for Being Convincing

1. Convince yourself first.
2. Be honest and sincere.
3. Don't exaggerate.
4. Inspire confidence for respect.
5. Relate to the other person. Be understanding.
6. Don't brag.
7. Speak moderately. Whispers can do more than shouts.
8. Practice reading aloud.
9. Don't parade your knowledge.
10. Be aggressive but not obnoxious.
11. Accept blame.
12. Improve your good qualities.
13. Consider the other person's feelings.
14. Know yourself to sell yourself.

7 Get Action!

The most important word in this book, I sincerely believe, is "ACTION." Without it nothing would ever have been started, nothing would ever have been completed, and nothing in the future will ever be accomplished. We can dream dreams of mighty magnitude, but without *action* we will face a stand-still future of no development, no more "magic"—no advancement comparable to radio, television, airplanes, electricity—just nothing new. Therefore, one cannot question the vital importance of "doing something about it"—whatever "it" may be!

Action invites the making of mistakes, but without them there would have been little progress in this world. The great achievements in every field of human endeavor since the dawn of time were built upon mistakes previously made. Thomas Edison built dozens of models of an electric

73

light over a two-year period before he got the filament to glow satisfactorily. Edgar Allan Poe submitted his manuscript for "The Raven" more than forty times before it was accepted by a publisher. Fifty years ago if anyone had argued in favor of attempting to land a human being on the moon he might have been placed in an asylum for the feebleminded! Even so simple a thing as an inkwell in a tube (the fountain pen) undoubtedly aroused laughter (and probably ruined a lot of shirts) before it was perfected. Whatever has been completed had to have a beginning—and seldom, if ever, was perfect at its inception.

So it's downright foolish to be "afraid to fail." Fear never won a battle! Indecision, doubt, and fear breed anxiety—and anxiety destroys mental and physical health, paralyzes your use of knowledge, neutralizes experience, strangles initiative, destroys skill, and stifles ingenuity. Anxiety is pain suffered for injuries that have not yet come, and that will probably never come. Imagination causes more disaster than reality!

Contrarily, courage is acquired by practicing courage. Courage is preserved by never surrendering to the things that rob you of courage. To overcome fear of failure, concentrate on important changes, ignore trivial ones. Forget about minor details, and never be afraid of cold hard facts. Too many great things have been accomplished after "experts" said they couldn't be done! Exercising your will power can give you confidence when you are right and can teach you valuable lessons when you are wrong.

Every victory over fear adds to your belief in yourself.

Nothing is more important than to live each day, not worrying about the past, and not anticipating worries in the future.

Figure out some answers for yourself after you have made mistakes; you may be wrong, but those "answers" show you're thinking. The right answers will surely restore your self-confidence.

The enemies of Action are Indifference and Inertia.

Indifference is the number-one obstacle you have to overcome in selling ANYTHING to ANYONE, whether it's your merchandise, your ideas or your personality; and when you begin to realize how terrific the competition is for the time and attention of others you begin to appreciate what a handicap indifference is!

Inertia is the law of physics that decrees that a body in motion, or at rest, resists change. People hate to bother changing their minds, their habits, their routines. They are worse than the buyer who won't talk; worse than those who fold their arms and say "make me laugh."

It takes a lot of persuasion to make people do even the things they *want* to do! That's why advertising does all sorts of things to get people to overcome that deadly enemy of action—Inertia.

Perhaps my own most important contribution to the advertising business was the invention of what I originally termed the "inertia plan." Like most inventions, mine was born of Mother "Necessity."

When the Book-of-the-Month Club was started, members had no idea what each forthcoming book of the month was until it was received—and too many books were returned as unsatisfactory. One day I suggested that we notify subscribers of the book selected before shipping it, giving them an honest review of it and telling them the book *would be sent unless within two weeks the form was returned notifying us* NOT *to send it*—or giving us an opportunity to send some substitute selection that we would also describe in the advance form. This is exactly what we did, and it turned out to be the "inertia plan" or "negative-option plan" now used by practically every book club, record club, and other of-the-month clubs around the world! And, it was all based on the plan that avoids the need for sending an order in every month or of renewing subscriptions when expired. One must ACT to change or cancel the terms of his original order.

How can this simple principle be applied to one's personal relationship with others, whether social or business? It depends upon what the relationship is. For example, a doctor, dentist, barber, or professional of any kind can make regular appointments automatic (unless canceled) without having to "sell" one every time a customer or client should be "treated." Appointments for regular visits can be made automatic for every week, every month, or every three months, or whatever interval is appropriate. If you are an office worker you might make arrangements for promotions or increases in salary at intervals that you think would be suitable to both you and your employer. If you purchase equipment of any kind and it should be regularly serviced, perhaps an arrangement can be made for it to be done on a regular monthly, quarterly, or semiannual basis.

The most important thing to consider is not to leave important matters dangling. Get them settled one way or another. Get the next meeting dated, if it is advisable to hold another meeting. At least leave word with your prospects that they will hear from you again within a specific time, or that if you do not hear from *them* by a certain date you will accept their silence as a positive answer. Instead of saying "Call me before Wednesday," say "Unless I hear from you by Wednesday I will assume you agree with me." There are many occasions to use this psychology. Silence can often mean consent in everyday arrangements, just as it regularly does in the "of-the-month" business.

Then there is the immature attitude of indecision. Living is coping with a combination of problems demanding action, and speculation that does not end in decision and activity is useless. It is tremendously important that you plan your course and act upon decisions at once. The old story of the mule that starved to death because he could not make up his mind which of the two stacks of straw to eat first is symbolic of people who never accomplish anything because they cannot make up their minds.

"Nothing ventured, nothing gained" is an old adage, just as true today as when first expressed. Before you can hope for success in any undertaking you must believe firmly that it is within your reach. To deny this is to admit defeat in advance. And the more frequently you deny yourself of the opportunity to "gamble" on your own ability, the more habitual failure becomes.

The reason we are "afraid to take a chance" is mainly because we are afraid we will fail! We are, therefore, afraid to make important decisions. Yet the most dangerous decision is to decide to make none at all! This is *advertising* of a negative nature, notifying all we meet that they cannot expect much from us.

You may excuse your own habit of avoiding the responsibility of making decisions by the ingrowing fear of making mistakes. But you will never overcome this fear by encouraging it. Whatever you are afraid of, whatever seem to be barriers to your happiness, you will find them relatively easy to overcome if you conquer them one at a time! If you suffer temporarily, you will be stronger and better able to cope with any difficulty the next time you face one. As for disappointments—think of the future, not of the past, and your battle will already be half won!

Successful personal salesmanship depends upon the salesman's ability to "close" whatever "deal" is being offered, to *complete* the sale. This "closing" cannot be accomplished by assuming a "take it or leave it" position.

Salesmen of all types of product have fought against this basic human inertia for many years. That is why in common everyday purchases we have so many "one-day" sales, "1¢" sales, "free premium" deals of all kinds, "only one to a customer" sales, and other inducements to *buy now*—not next week or tomorrow, but *now*—TODAY—

sometimes even limited to hours BEFORE NOON, or restricted in other ways.

In your daily dealings with others you are frequently called upon to make decisions that are important to you at once but that may not become effective for weeks or even months ahead. So you delay deciding. Why hurry? You'll think about it. You'll discuss it with so-and-so. Yes, you know you need it, but you want to think it over. These delays may be fatal to your "sale." The farther away your prospect moves from you physically or mentally the more remote are your chances of getting the order.

Meet the challenge of the old axiom: "Actions speak louder than words." Promises may be encouraging but they will not butter your bread today, nor will they enable you to take the long-hoped-for vacation! So, figuratively speaking, have your order blank handy, your pen or pencil poised, ready to record your customer's commitment to action. And always behave as if you EXPECT acceptance, not denial, of your proposition.

Always strive to get a "yes" or a "no" decision on any request or proposal you may have made. Don't leave matters hanging in the air. Remember, the motivating word is ACTION. This habit should become so much a part of your life that it will come into play whatever your problem may be. It can help you to be punctual for your appointments, help you to choose your investments, help you to decide whether to move to a new home or remain where you are. It will enable you to pinpoint an aim in your conversation, in your writing, even in your own mind as to what you want your customer or prospect to do or think.

Many years ago, when Listerine was advertised as a fine mouthwash, its sales had reached a certain point and leveled off. But when it was advertised "as a remedy for halitosis"—even though its use was a confession on the part of the purchaser that he or she was a victim of bad breath—its sales vaulted. This may seem a far cry from advertising yourself, but upon careful analysis you may find that you have certain traits that could, if honestly and frankly advertised, benefit your prospective "customer" and help him solve a problem.

The secret of securing *action* from a "prospect" is to emphasize the benefits that will accrue to him if he "acts now." His first "objection" is usually a reluctance to spend the time, money, or effort on anything new to him. Second, but not usually recognized, is his feeling of loyalty to those who have been "calling" on him for months or years before you came along. Next, he hates to admit that he has been *sold* instead of thinking of himself as being a buyer. He wants to feel the decision was his.

The answer to most of these "objections" is to make your prospect feel that he is getting the best of the bargain. You should earnestly try to make the "other fellow"—whether your boss, your wife, your husband, your banker, or whoever—fully aware that you are being generous and that he or she is being understanding and appreciative. You cannot afford to offer an "even trade." You *must* give your "prospect" the feeling of facing an opportunity by acting at once to obtain a worthwhile "bargain" whatever it is you are "selling." If the "buyer" sees no advantage in dealing with you, why should he change his "source of supply"? That is why so many advertisers offer special inducements and promises to get "action" from prospects they have "convinced" but who will not be customers until they actually "buy and try" at the supplier's expense or partly so. Read the ads and see how many "special offers" are made by even the most respected stores. They know the value of initial sales. They want *action,* not merely reputation!

For the sake of your future do not bury your ideas, or "save" them for "sometime later." If you are capable of original thinking you will be rewarded by good new ideas as rapidly as you can use them. Don't be afraid someone will steal your idea—if anyone does, you will think of a better one soon. Talk modestly about your ideas to impress your listeners, whether or not they "buy" your thinking. Many times you will discover your ideas of months or years ago adopted and marketed—frequently unsuccessfully, by someone unable to keep pace with the consequences of your original idea. There is nothing like positive action to put negative thoughts to flight. Your whole mind should turn to thoughts of success; then thoughts of failure and fears of what may occur will melt like darkness before a rising sun. Imagine what a backward world this would be if it were not for people who ACTED upon their ideas instead of putting them off from day to day, year to year.

The greatest handicap to anyone's progress is underestimating one's own abilities. As the old saying goes, "How do you know you can't do it unless you *try*?" And even if you've tried and failed, have you remembered, "If at first you don't succeed, try, try, again"? The history of every great accomplishment is strewn with examples of early failure and long struggle, from biblical times to the space age. But the Israelites *did* emerge from the wilderness, and man *did* land on the moon!

Everyone in the course of his lifetime fails to make good on some promises and resolutions. Give them another try. See if now, in possession of greater strength and experience, you can fulfill your promises and wipe the slate clean.

Even if you're sure you can't do it, try again. Even if it's never been done before, even if it's been laughed at by "wiseacres," try it. Since you've admitted it can't be done, you have nothing to lose. Many a person standing still because something "couldn't be done" has been brushed aside by someone who was doing it. So try something new. Use your imagination. Maybe the impossible requires a new technique, a new attitude on your part. Try it, it may work! Even if it's "impossible," try it. Trying helps you discover hundreds of new things that you *can* do. It revitalizes your imagination. So TRY IT! Don't give up to the other fellow. Even if you're tired, weary, discouraged, "broke," TRY SOMETHING YOU'VE ALWAYS THOUGHT OF TRYING! The best time to try is when you don't feel like doing it. More thinking, more work, and less talk accomplish what later on seem to be miracles. If you have a number of problems to solve, start by tackling the one you can surely beat, then

82

go on to the next easier one, and when you get to the hardest one, it won't be so difficult as it seemed.

Choose the problem that in your judgment is within your limits; mobilize the energy necessary for working out a solution; stick to your purpose despite temporary discouragement. If you cannot solve your easiest problem, certainly you cannot solve your most difficult one. Every day do at least one thing for no other reason than that you don't feel like doing it.

To advertise yourself *to others,* begin by advertising yourself TO YOU! When you have made *that* sale you will find it easier by far than you ever dreamed it would be to ADVERTISE YOURSELF— and to SELL YOURSELF to the rest of the "market" that needs the REAL YOU!

Checklist for Getting Action

1. Do something about "it." *Action* is necessary!
2. Don't bury your ideas.
3. Don't be afraid to make mistakes. Analyze and learn from them.
4. Don't be one of the mob.
5. Practice self-confidence.
6. Indifference and inertia are obstacles. Overcome them.
7. Take a chance. It's a way of learning.
8. Don't leave things in midair. Make a decision.
9. Nothing ventured, nothing gained; so TRY!

8
Conclusion

Advertising, obviously, has its limitations. The story told about a manufacturer of a widely used product sold in drugstores is a good example. Of course, it's only a fanciful story, but it serves to illustrate just how far advertising "experts" may sometimes wander to "sell" products.

It seems that in this manufacturer's hometown a tremendous effort was being made to raise enough money to build an observatory for the local stargazers. When asked by the fundraising committee for a large contribution, the manufacturer snorted a violent "no!" But after much pleading, he gave in, and pledged a substantial amount *if* the authorities would agree to rearrange the stars across the heavens so that they would spell out, every night for an hour, the name of his product—which happened to be a very famous laxative!

85

There are many kinds of advertising that do not apply to many kinds of merchandise. Radio, television, skywriting, magazines, newspapers, billboard posters—I could go on indefinitely; but to be effective the advertising must first of all be JUSTIFIED in the eyes of the public. It must have character, an unquestionable honesty, a genuine "excuse for existence": it should serve a real purpose for the benefit of the public to be most effective.

And so it is with our own personal advertising. We need not become stars in the sky or thunder and lightning, or scorching heat or numbing cold. We should be sunshine and warmth and extend a generally pleasant welcome to all we meet.

The beginning of good personal advertising is the realization that common courtesy is the most inexpensive advertising we can do for ourselves.

Courtesy is a mark of good breeding. It is a recognition of the rights of others. To be courteous is to practice the Golden Rule. To be discourteous is to be brutal, self-centered, intolerant—the very opposite of good personal advertising. Courtesy costs nothing, but it adds so much to whatever anyone is "selling" that it seems criminal ever to neglect it.

Businesses are often built on courteous conversation with customer, employer, or client. Some can honestly say we are in the business of creating favorable impressions—but all of us are in the people-to-people business.

The first and best place to practice courtesy is at home. We naturally incline to be more polite with total strangers

86

than with those who are near and dear to us, yet we must know that our loved ones will appreciate our courtesy even more than strangers. Try courtesy on your husband or wife; try it on your kids! You'll be amazed at how happy your home can be! If you practice courtesy at home it will become second nature, and after that you will regard a discourteous act of your own as the worst mistake you can make wherever you may be!

So, to my mind, the first principle of being a successful advertising person is to treat everyone you meet as if he were a long-lost rich relative—no matter how unimpressive he may look, dress, or talk. The importance of a smile, a gracious greeting, a kind word, real courtesy—all the way from the parking lot attendant to the president of your bank—and ESPECIALLY IN YOUR OWN HOME cannot be overlooked. You can never be "too busy," "too poor," "too rich," too tired," or too anything else *to be courteous*! It's the cheapest form of advertising known!

The wisdom of the late Bernard Baruch helped shape the destiny of many a man—and many a nation. If we could sit down with him today, this is the counsel he would give us—as he gave it to the world during his lifetime. He called it his "recipe for success." There are fifteen ingredients:

(1) *Be polite*. (2) Prepare yourself for whatever you are asked to do. (3) Keep yourself tidy. (4) Be cheerful. (5) Don't be envious. (6) Be honest with yourself so you will be honest with others. (7) Be helpful.

87

(8) Interest yourself in your job. (9) Don't pity yourself. (10) Be quick to praise. (11) Be loyal to your friends. (12) Avoid prejudices. (13) Be independent. (14) Interest yourself in politics. (15) Read the newspapers.

All the ingredients in Baruch's "recipe" are important, but remember that the *first* is "Be polite."

Some of us are "born bookkeepers," some are "born writers," others are "born lawyers," still others are "born nobodies." Whatever you want to be but are not or think you cannot be, you should aim to join. If you are strong in one area of human accomplishment, keep going in that area and connect with someone who is strong in the area where you are weak! Don't try to learn to do everything yourself! The surest sign of strength is to admit your weaknesses. Advertise your strength by admitting that you "don't know it all," by asking questions of those who specialize in the areas where you know you are not qualified to make sound decisions. Every great man in history became great because he specialized—even if his specialty was asking others (who knew more) what the answers were to certain problems.

Don't feel "stuck up" about every argument you seem to "win." Don't allow yourself the luxury of reveling in your minor accomplishments. And when you fail, just keep going; and deny yourself the time it takes to feel blue.

The quickest way to achieve success, happiness, and peace of mind is to keep busy doing what comes naturally.

88

We are all born with certain talents that, when translated into a gainful occupation, can make it easy for us to compete favorably with others similarly talented. Modesty can be just as much abused by having too much of it as by having too little of it. If you sow seeds of self-doubt, you will reap a harvest of fears and indecisions. Take stock of yourself and conclude that "I'm not such a dud after all."

All the precepts in the systems manuals are worthless unless you have the spirit to make them work. Emerson put it into a line: "Nothing great was ever achieved without enthusiasm." One's spirits rise when action starts, and there is a feeling of zest. Enthusiasm is doing things, not talking about them.

To get from paper plans to action one must commit oneself. It is unjust and unreasonable to be unwilling to pay this price. Performance, however short of perfection, is better than promise without effort. Group your activities so that one follows another with least disruption and effort. If you have a job to do, dig up the necessary facts before starting work on it. Whatever task is before you, think it through from beginning to end before you start.

Eventually, despite all the examples set before you daily, you will have to gamble on your own judgment. You MUST learn to trust yourself. The important thing is to start NOW!

It is entirely up to you to get the most out of life with whatever assets you possess—and to increase your assets whenever and however you can, in order to aid you in reaching your goal.

Keep these five essential requirements of successful advertising in your mind every day, all day, every week, all year and you'll get the most out of your PERSONAL ADVERTISING:

1. KNOW YOUR MERCHANDISE (YOURSELF)
2. ATTRACT FAVORABLE ATTENTION
3. KEEP 'EM INTERESTED
4. BE CONVINCING
5. GET ACTION!

Acknowledgments

As I have frequently and proudly stated, the first book I ever read on the subject of advertising was written by Professor Walter Dill Scott of Northwestern University. I not only read it, I revered it, devoured it, followed its teachings as closely as I could with what intelligence I possessed. I have had Professor Scott's book since 1908—and still have it! What amazes me even more today, *nearly seventy years later,* is how a college professor, a psychologist, could possibly know so much about *advertising* as to have written such a marvelous textbook.

This then is my apology for presenting this book! As an advertising man I have gleaned many thoughts from the works of college professors, psychologists, authors, historians. A partial list of those I have read while preparing this book follows. I thank the authors for their guidance.

HOW TO ADVERTISE YOURSELF

BENNETT, MILLARD. *The Power of Inspired Salesmanship.* New York: Frederick Fell, Inc., 1960.

CAPLES, JOHN. *Tested Advertising Methods.* Englewood Cliffs, N.J.: Prentice-Hall, Inc., 1974.

DAVIDSON, SOL M. *The Cultivation of Imperfection.* New York: Frederick Fell, Inc., 1965.

LAVIDGE, ARTHUR W. *A Common-Sense Guide to Professional Advertising.* Blue Ridge Summit, Penn.: TAB Books, 1973.

MANGAN, JAMES T. *How To Win Self-Confidence for Selling.* Englewood Cliffs, N.J.: Prentice-Hall, Inc., 1957.

MARATTA, JAMES T. *Brainwashing Is a Cinch!* New York: Vantage Press, Inc., 1966

MARTINEAU, PIERRE. *Motivation in Advertising.* New York: McGraw-Hill Book Co., Inc., 1957.

MISSILDINE, W. HUGH, AND GALTON, LAWRENCE. *Your Inner Conflicts: How To Solve Them.* New York: Simon & Schuster, Inc., 1974.

OSBORN, ALEX. *Wake Up Your Mind.* New York: Charles Scribner's Sons, 1952.

OVERSTREET, H. A. *About Ourselves.* New York: W. W. Norton & Co., Inc., 1927.

SCOTT, WALTER DILL. *The Psychology of Advertising.* Boston: Small, Maynard & Co., 1908.

Beyond all this I thank Ms. Julia Zack for her help and patience in researching, typing, retyping, and editing the material contained herein, and my wife Mary for her cooperation while this book was being written.

92